ב"ה

לה' הארץ ומלואה

This book belongs to

_____

_____

_____

To our dear children,
who have taught us so much,
and helped us discover and
enjoy all that Hashem
has given to us.

Yehuda and the Rain in the Succah
Part of the Jewish Discovery Series

First Edition - Elul 5783 / September 2023
Copyright © 2023 by Amsy Books Limited
ALL RIGHTS RESERVED

ISBN: 978-1-9164311-1-9

Published by:
Targum Publishers
Shlomo ben Yosef 131a/1
Jerusalem 9380581
editor@targumpublishers.com

Distributed by:
Ktav Publishers & Distributors Inc.
527 Empire Blvd.
Brooklyn, NY 11225-3121
Tel: 718-972-5449, 201-963-9524
Fax: 718-972-6307, 201-963-0102
www.ktav.com

Also in The Jewish Discovery Series
Yisroel and the Pesach Salt Water
Tova and the Shavuos Ice Pops

www.jewishdiscoveryseries.com

Printed in Israel

Yehuda
and the
Rain in the Succah

By Chaviva Pink
Illustrated by Racheli David

Yehuda woke up early in the morning. He felt excited. Today was special, but he could not remember why. What could today be, he wondered?

Yehuda heard a loud banging noise coming from outside his window. He said *modeh ani*, washed *negel vasser* and jumped out of bed.

When Yehuda looked out of the window, what did he see? He saw Tatty building the *Succah*.

Now Yehuda remembered why he was so excited... today is *Erev Succos*. Tonight would be the first night of *Succos*.

A huge smile was on Yehuda's face as he made his bed, emptied his *negel vasser*, and got dressed.

Yehuda ran down the stairs singing a *Succos* song that he had learned in school.

"Good morning, Mommy", said Yehuda.

Mommy gave Yehuda a big hug, held his hands and started dancing around the kitchen.

Mommy and Yehuda laughed and danced around so much that they were totally out of breath.

"Do you know why I am so excited today? asked Mommy

Yehuda knew! "It's because tonight is *Succos*", he replied.

"Yes that's right. We have so many special *mitzvos* to do today, to get ready for *Succos* tonight. Let's *daven* and eat breakfast. Then we will be ready to begin", said Mommy.

Everything was ready for *Succos* to begin. Everyone was dressed in their *Yom Tov* clothes. Yehuda couldn't wait for his cousins Gavi and Rivka to come and eat the *Yom Tov* meal together with them tonight.

Mommy and Yehuda's sister Leah lit the *Yom Tov* candles.

Tatty, Yehuda and his brother Zalman went to *shul*.

After *Shul*, Tatty, Yehuda and Zalman walked home with their cousins.

Yehuda looked up at the sky. Uh, oh! It was full of clouds. Is it going to rain tonight in our *Succah*, wondered Yehuda?

When they arrived home, Mommy opened the door. "Good *Yom Tov!* Let's go into the *Succah*."

Tatty made *Kiddush* and *Hamotzei* and everyone enjoyed the sweet wine and *challah*.

After eating the fish course, Mommy served soup and *kneidelach* to everyone.

As Yehuda was eating his favourite food, *kneidelach*, he thought he heard something. He stopped eating and listened. "Is that rain I hear?" he asked.

Just then, splash! A rain drop fell right into Yehuda's soup. Then another rain drop fell into Zalman's soup. Everyone started laughing.

The rain got heavier and heavier. Soon everyone had rain drops falling into their soup.

"Quick," said Tatty. "Let's finish our soup and go wait inside until the rain stops."

Everyone went inside. They stood at the window watching the rain.

Yehuda looked at his Tatty and asked, "Tatty, where does rain come from?'

Tatty smiled at Yehuda. "Wow, that's a great question.

"Rain comes from Hashem. Hashem created an amazing way for the rain to fall from the sky. This is called the **water cycle.**

"Let me explain to you how it works."

Yehuda, Zalman, Leah, Gavi and Rivka sat down to listen to Tatty.

"The water cycle is made up of three main parts."

1

"The first part of the water cycle is called **evaporation**."

Tatty explained, "When the sun shines, it warms up the water in rivers, lakes and oceans".

"And puddles?" asked Yehuda.

"That's right!" Tatty continued. "The sun turns the warmed up water into **vapour** or **steam**.

"If you watch a kettle boil, the water will get hotter and hotter. You will notice that **vapour** or **steam** comes out of the spout."

"Like the **steam** coming out of the pot when Mommy boils pasta?" asked Yehuda.

"Exactly," answered Tatty. "The **vapour** or **steam** leaves the rivers, lakes, oceans or puddles and goes into the air. This is called **evaporation**.

2

"The second part of the water cycle is called **condensation**.

"**Condensation** is when the vapour or steam that has gone into the air cools down. This changes the vapour or steam back into little droplets of water. These little droplets of water make clouds.

3

"The third part of the water cycle is called **precipitation**.

When lots of water has condensed into clouds, the clouds become very heavy. The air cannot hold these heavy clouds any more.

"The water from the clouds falls down to the ground. This is called **precipitation**.

"**Precipitation** can be rain, snow, sleet or hail.

"When the **precipitation** has reached the ground, it collects in the oceans, lakes, rivers and puddles.

"Hashem is so kind. He makes water fall in the perfect way so:

"Children can drink water.

"Birds can drink water.

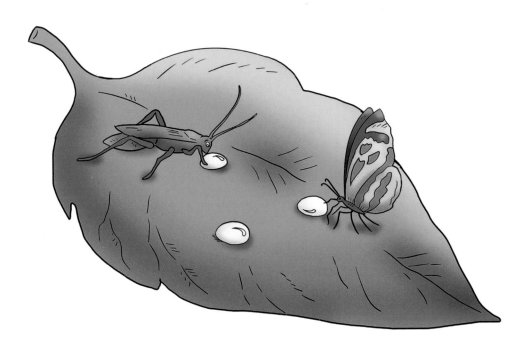

"Insects can drink water.

"Plants, trees and flowers can drink water.

The children were amazed that such a *nes* happens every time it rains.

"Round and round and round the water goes." said Yehuda.

"Hey, it's stopped raining!" exclaimed Zalman.
"Yay! Let's go back into the *Succah* for the rest of our meal."

As Yehuda walked back to the *Succah*, he was thinking about the warm sun that would shine tomorrow and the water cycle that would start all over again.

"Good night clouds.
We love it when the rain falls on the ground.
But please wait till *Succos* is not around."

Glossary:

Modeh Ani – The prayer we say after waking up to thank Hashem for returning our souls to us.

Negel Vasser – lit. "nail water" - washing our hands right after saying *modeh ani*.

Succah – A hut built for the *Yom Tov* of *Succos*.

Yom Tov - Jewish holiday.

Mitzvah – Commandment from the *Torah*.

Daven – Pray.

Erev Succos – The day before *Succos*.

Challah – Bread loaves eaten at *Shabbos* and *Yom Tov* meals.

Kiddush – A blessing made over the wine on *Shabbos* and *Yom Tov*.

Hamotzi – The blessing made over the *challah*.

Kneidelach – Matzah balls eaten with soup.

Nes - Miracle

Experiment Activity

We want to find out:

How is rain made?

You will need:

- 1 glass that can hold boiling water
- 1 small plate
- 6 ice cubes
- Hot water
- Kettle

Instructions:

WARNING: *This experiment must be done with an adult because you need to use boiling water.*

1) Boil water in the kettle.

2) Pour the boiling water into the glass until the glass is half full.

3) Quickly put the plate on top of the glass of boiling water.

4) Let the plate sit there for 30-40 seconds.

5) Take the ice cubes and place them on top of the plate.

Results:

- Some of the water in the glass evaporates.
- It rises in the glass as steam, *(evaporation)* until it hits the cold plate.
- When the warm steam hits the cold plate it cools down and condenses *(condensation)*.
- This turns into rain.
- Watch as the rain slides down the glass *(precipitation)*.

Extra Activity:

Can you think of any other experiments that you can do that will produce condensation or precipitation?

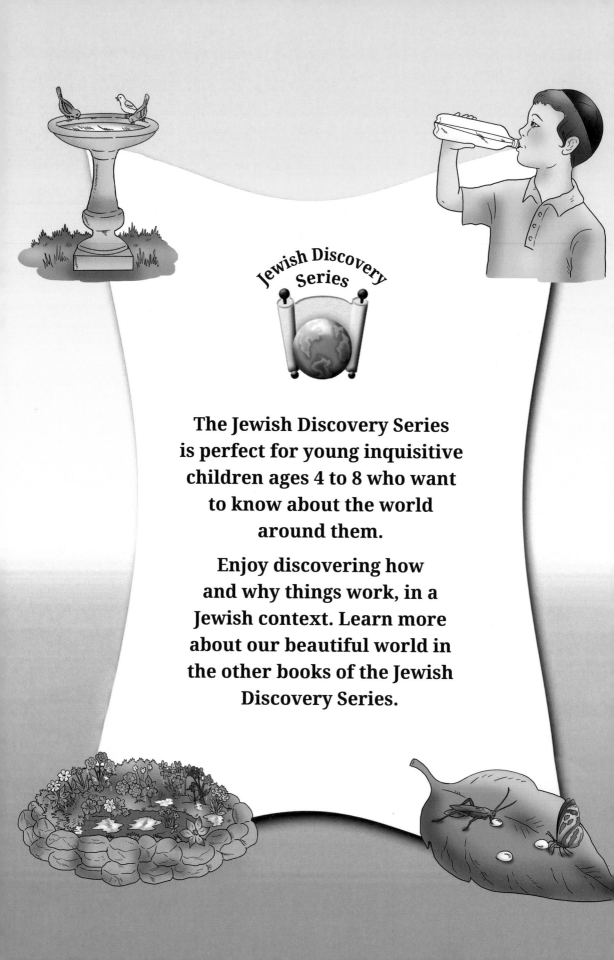

Jewish Discovery Series

The Jewish Discovery Series
is perfect for young inquisitive
children ages 4 to 8 who want
to know about the world
around them.

Enjoy discovering how
and why things work, in a
Jewish context. Learn more
about our beautiful world in
the other books of the Jewish
Discovery Series.